QUESTIONS
Singles & Youth
ask about
RELATIONSHIP/ COURTSHIP

OLUWABUNMI F. AKANO

QUESTIONS SINGLES AND YOUTH ASKED ABOUT RELATIONSHIP
Copyright © 2021 by Oluwabunmi F. Akano

All rights reserved. No part of this publication may be reproduced, distributed, or transmitted in any form or by any means, including photocopying, recording, or other electronic or mechanical methods, without the prior written permission of the publisher or author, except in the case of brief quotations embodied in critical reviews and certain other noncommercial uses permitted by copyright law.

Although every precaution has been taken to verify the accuracy of the information contained herein, the author and publisher assume no responsibility for any errors or omissions. No liability is assumed for damages that may result from the use of information contained within.

ISBN-13:   Paperback: 978-1-64749-339-4

Printed in the United States of America

GoToPublish LLC
1-888-337-1724
www. Gotopublish. Com
info@gotopublish. Com

CONTENTS

INTRODUCTION 1
WHAT IS COURTSHIP? 2
DIFFERENCES BETWEEN COURTSHIP
AND DATING 4
WHO IS THE ORIGINATOR OF COURTSHIP? 5
WHAT IS THE PURPOSE OF COURTSHIP? 6
WHY DO I NEED A SELF-EXAMINATION? 7
WHY IS COURTSHIP IMPORTANT? 15
WHAT IS THE DURATION FOR COURTSHIP? 17
HOW MANY TIMES CAN I GO THROUGH
COURTSHIP 19
BEFORE MARRIAGE?
WHY DO I NEED TO ABSTAIN FROM
SEX(FORNICATION) 20
BEFORE MARRIAGE?
WHAT ARE THE PREVENTIVE MEASURES
AGAINST FORNICATION? 21
ARE THERE REMEDIES FOR ME WHO
ALREADY HAD SEX BEFORE MARRIAGE? 23
MORE QUESTIONS TO ASK. 24
CONCLUSION. 34

ACKNOWLEDGEMENTS

WITH SPECIAL THANKS:

. Firstly, goes to God almighty who gave me the inspiration and the power to be able to accomplish this book.

. To my dear husband, Pastor Kayode Akano, for his love, patient, understanding, prayer and support.

. To my children, Oluwatamilore, Toluwanimi and Oluwatoni for being there for me.

. To my honorable nieces, Christina and Racheal Obadare, for their time spent reading and supporting me.

. To Pastor Sam Obadare, Evangelist Oluwatoyin Akinfeleye for your prayers and encouraging words and support.

.To Pastor Abraham and Evangelist Esther Obadare, for your time, encouragement and the efforts you put to make sure this book is published, I am grateful.

DEDICATION

This book is dedicated to all singles and youth all over the world, who want their relationship to work and have a happy married life.

INTRODUCTION

Questions upon questions needing urgent, correct answers run through the mind of the youths and singles who are interested in having a healthy relationship and how to maintain it. For example, how do I understand my partner in my relationship? How and when do I express my feelings to my partner without being offensive? Why do I need to go through courtship and what do I need to do to keep my relationship flourishing etc.?

This book is about giving right answers to the questions in your mind. By the grace of God, I hope by the time you are done reading this book you will be satisfied with the answers you need. These answers have been gathered from the Holy Bible, one on one interaction with certain people whose relationships or marriages are successful and from reliable sources. Some of these questions are collected from both young and old, single and married, audios and books.

God is interested in our relationship (dating, courtship and marriage), therefore we are to take them seriously. God instituted marriage from the beginning in the garden of Eden. He created it for companionship, love, support, sharing, respect for each other, enjoyment and blessing but not the way marriage is handled today. I would like to dwell more on courtship in this book.

Courtship is important and necessary for partners who want to settle down and have a good marriage. There is no sense in rushing into marriage without adequate knowledge and preparation for it. That is why it is important to be wise so that your marriage doesn't end tragically and suddenly.

Reading this book will enlighten you on the process of courtship and inform you what to look out for during courtship. It also clears the misconceptions about courting and dating. God bless as you read.

WHAT IS COURTSHIP?

1. It is the stage where friends who find themselves attracted to one another agree to take their friendship to the next level.

2. It is a period to discover if you can be equally yoked with your partner forever (2 Corinthians 6:14) spiritually, mentally, emotionally and socially.

3. It is dating with a purpose of exploring all aspects of life with your partner without the complexity of being intimate sexually until marriage.

4. It's a time to be convinced enough without any doubt that the partner you have chosen is the right one you want to live with for the rest of your life, create a family, build a life of trust and future together.

5. It is also a preparation time for a life-time commitment, that is, marriage. Here you will be taught and understand what marriage is about and all that it entails. For example, two of you becoming one after marriage meaning no more i, me and myself but we. Making decisions together, plan and adjust together and much more.

Based on the meaning of courtship, then as a child of God you are not to go into any relationship with the opposite gender until you have prayed and are very sure that God is the one leading you. Also, you should not commit to a relationship for the fun of it, or because others are doing it. Do not allow yourself to be forced into a relationship when you are not ready.

DIFFERENCES BETWEEN COURTSHIP AND DATING

Partners dating may not have any specific expectations for their relationship except those that seek God before starting.

Relationships in dating may not be well defined while in courting it is well defined.

Plans may or may not be visible in dating, but plans are well laid in courtship.

In dating they may just be having fun and still seeking where the relationship will lead to.

Dating may be to look for someone to just spend a short time with and move on, while courtship is looking for a long-time partner to spend the rest of their time with.

Dating may not have serious attachment while courtship is a true commitment.

In dating the feeling of love (and sometimes lust) is stressed while spiritual health is not promoted but in courtship, discipline and godly character are considered along with love (2cor 6:9-10)

Physical attraction is prioritized more in dating while in courtship spiritual attraction is prioritized.

Self-centered approach (Philippian 3:18-19, 1 John 2:15-17,) thinking what they feel is right in dating but in courtship God-centered approach is carried out (Romans 6:11, 2 Corinthians 5:15).

While in some people's practices, dating allows for multiple concurrent relationships - a practice which is neither right nor biblical-, courtship strictly involves only one partner at a time, to focus on the relationship.

The risk of hurt, heartbreaks and scars are more evident in dating than in courtship.

WHO IS THE ORIGINATOR OF COURTSHIP?

God is the Originator of family relationships which, biblically, starts with man and woman; and He is interested and concerned about how we handle it. In Genesis, God created the relationship between man and woman in the garden of Eden. He created them for companionship, support, communion and intimacy. This is the reason we must involve God first before we go into it. We must pray to seek His instructions and be led by Him. The word "Partner" as used in this book refers to either a male involved in a relationship with a female or a female involved in a relationship with a male.

WHAT IS THE PURPOSE OF COURTSHIP?

It is important to know the actual purpose of going through the process of courtship. Therefore, the purposes of courtship are:

- To grow and nourish love or perhaps "interest" with a view towards marriage.
- To give time to assess and evaluate compatibility as lifelong marriage partners.
- To find answers to some personal and pertinent questions that each may have about their partner and their relationship.
- To be able to express their concerns to each other about their similarities and differences and how they can work them out
- To discover some of their strengths and weaknesses and how they can strengthen their weaknesses and compliment their strengths to achieve a good and healthy marriage.
- To be able to work out things between them as one such as planning and decision making.

WHY DO I NEED SELF-EXAMINATION?

Examining yourself will help you determine if you are ready to continue in the relationship or you need more time. To help you discover if you have the right attitude or mindset towards yourself and marriage. In addition, it will help you to define why you want to go ahead with this person. Here are few questions listed below to help you in your self-examination:

- **HOW IS MY RELATIONSHIP WITH GOD AND HAVE I ASKED HIM ABOUT MY RELATIONSHIP WITH THE OTHER PERSON?** How smooth is your relationship with God? Your relationship with God comes first (Matthew 6:33) and every other relationship is built on it. Having constant fellowship with God. Creating time to study the word of God (Joshua 1:8) and praying without ceasing (1 Thessalonians 5:16). Being connected with God for his counselling and wisdom to handle your life and relationship rightly is very important. Asking Him for direction and support that you might also need after the confirmation from God is very necessary.

- **AM I GOING INTO A RELATIONSHIP THINKING I CAN CHANGE THE OTHER PERSON?** It is a wrong mindset to go into a relationship with the thought that you can change your partner. It is only God that has that power to change anybody in terms of their character, mentality or belief, you can only give advice or support and pray for the other person. It is better to work and change yourself for the better than trying to change someone else. Have a positive and right mindset about yourself, people and things and reduce or do away with negative thoughts.

- **AM I CONTENTED OR GREEDY PERSON?** The Bible says contentment with godliness is a great gain. You must be satisfied with the ones you have and learn to appreciate them. Don't be greedy for someone else's things. If any help is rendered to you or gifts are given to you, you must appreciate them rather than complaining. Although man's wants are numerous and insatiable, we must still learn to be grateful for the ones we have and thanking God of provision. This will help you in your relationship not to be a complainer, frustrated or pushy person when your needs are not met immediately or are met halfway.

- **AM I A HUMBLE OR PRIDEFUL PERSON?** The Bible says, pride goes before a fall. God hates a prideful person but the humble He exalt. Are you someone who is humble, respectful and regards people no matter their status, age or gender? You must be humble to say sorry when you offend others or at fault.

- **AM I A FAITHFUL OR UNFAITHFUL PERSON?** The Bible says, if you are faithful in little things, God will commit bigger things in your hands. Be faithful in all your dealings and be transparent. Let your loyalty lie in that person who committed that thing to you. Do everything given to you with all diligence and with all honesty. Always stand for the truth.

- **AM I A JOYFUL OR SAD PERSON?** A person has a great influence on himself/herself and the environment. If you are someone who is always joyful, you make people and your environment the same but if you are always a sad person you can easily pollute the environment and the people there with your sadness. Most times we have a great influence on how our environment should be and the kind of people we want around us. If you are the person with a happy face people will love to associate, be around you but if you are the opposite then you need to amend your ways. Do not let material things determine your joy but God. In good or bad times, in need or not, be full of joy and believing in God that will keep you going on in life.

- **DO I CARE, LOVE AND SHOW KINDNESS?** Do you love and care for yourself and others or for yourself alone (me, I and myself). The Bible says care for one another and look out for each other. The Bible also states that love your neighbor as yourself. My question is, do you love and care for yourself? Do you care about the actions you take, how you look, how you take care of yourself financially, spiritually, emotionally? How do you want people to treat you? You must first love, care and be kind to yourself before you can express them to others. What you do not have you cannot give. For instance, if you do not treat yourself with respect you cannot respect others too. Love is about give and take.

    If you hate yourself and go into a relationship without dealing with it, it will affect your relationship badly. Some hate themselves because of the bad experience they had in the past like some being molested from their past, some being used and dumped in a relationship. But whatever the reason maybe, you need to seek help to get rid of the hate before going into a relationship. You need God to forgive yourself and anyone who had hurt you, you need God to help you overcome the past to move on, you need to talk about it to someone with who is God fearing and you need counselling.

- **HOW DO I HANDLE MY PHYSICAL APPEARANCE?** Take good care of your body and clothes. Be your best in appearance always and do not overdo it. Makeup was known then to enhance beauty but now people change their outlook totally, so make up but don't overdo it. The Bible says let your moderation be known to all. Let your appearance be modest and moderate. Let your dressing be appropriate and not expose the part of your body that needs to be covered up. Accept and be happy for the way God has created you. Don't be someone else. Appreciate who you are. the right person for you will also appreciate you.

- **AM I A HONEST AND TRUTHFUL PERSON?** Be truthful and honest to God, yourself and people around you. How good are you in listening and taking the truth? Don't hide your feelings, in truthful and honesty with humility express your feelings about a situation or what your thoughts are. Be free and not be timid or afraid to share your opinion. This allows people around you to be honest and free to express their feelings to you.

AM I OPEN MINDED FOR DISCUSSION AND COMMUNICATION? It is wrong to assume that people should understand when you never communicated (by talking) nothing to them. Communication is an important key in a healthy relationship. You should know what, when, where and how to communicate with people. Create avenues for discussion and avoid arguments, complaining, murmuring. Try to make your points clear without accusation and if you do not understand the person ask questions. Be a person who is ready to learn new good things. Be ready for change where necessary and not be a rigid or resistant person. Be open minded to take criticism, correction and compliment.

- **DO I TREAT MY RELATIONSHIP WITH ALL SERIOUSNESS AND GENTLENESS?** Take everything about you with all seriousness and not take them for granted. Treat your relationship with all seriousness but gentleness at the same time. Put in your hard work and your best, with all diligence, love and care in everything you do. Do not rush yourself into doing anything, take your time to make it work.

- **DO I KNOW MY WEAKNESSES AND STRENGTHS?** Try to know your own strength and use it to your advantage while you work on your weakness.
- **DO I RUSH TO JUDGE, CRITICIZE OR CONDEMN?** Without thorough investigation and not giving a benefit of doubt for the other person to explain, it is wrong to rush to judge a person or their action. Search all things to know and hold the truth before you jump to conclusions about a matter. Do not point accusing fingers and create unnecessary fights. For example, a friend gives you a call that she saw your partner at McDonald with another female eating together. First and foremost, you do not know who that female is to him, maybe his relations who just branch at

his office or his business associate. Therefore, you need to cool yourself down from anger and not rush to judgement. secondly pray to God for patience and wisdom to handle the issue in the right way with him. Then when you meet do not confront him first with all the questions about the issue, try and talk about how he is and everything else. Then calmly and politely ask him the case you heard and give him the opportunity to explain. From his reaction and explanations, you will be able to know if he is telling the truth or not.

- **HAVE I BROADEN MY HORIZON?** Be versatile, learn and read other stuff apart from your professional stuff. Broaden your mind about other topics such as politics, religion and social activities. This will help you to associate and feel comfortable when among other people.

- **SHOULD I AVOID TALKING ABOUT SEX?** When you are with your partner avoid talking about your sexual feelings to prevent temptation and falling into sin (fornication) or prevent yourself from defiling your marital bed before marriage.

- **SHOULD I AVOID TALKING ABOUT MY EXES?** It is important to note that it is wrong to keep bringing up exes in your relationship to prevent an uncomfortable environment for your partner, to avoid jealousy and mistrust. Build the confidence in your partner that you are done with the past. Do not let your past hinder you from making positive decisions in your life but learn from the past and ask God to help you move on with your life.

- **DO I TREAT MY COURTSHIP LIKE A JOB?** Your relationship is not a job where you are only interested in interviewing your partner every time. Be creative with your time together as well like having fellowship with one another, visiting places, watching movies, just to mention a few of things you can do together. discover what you can do and achieve together.

- **DO I SEEK THE COUNSEL OF THE WISE PEOPLE?** You must be someone who seeks the Lord for counsel. Also asking wise parents, men and women of God older than you and wise friends in Christ for counselling is a good idea. Seek counsel from those who derive their wisdom from God and His Word.

- **WHAT KIND OF RELATIONSHIP DO I HAVE WITH YOUR PARENTS AND SIBLINGS?** The way you relate to your mother and sisters as a guy will be the same way you are likely to behave to your partner when you marry her. Similarly, the way a female behaves towards her father and brother is the same way she will behave towards her husband. For example, if she is rude and disrespectful to her father she is going to treat her husband the same. I will advise that you treat your family with kindness and love. Let your family be your number one priority before your friends. Treat them right. Before you jump to conclusions about your partner it is good to examine yourself too to find out if you are the one who needs to work on or your partner.

Doing intentional self-introspection and examination is healthy for a good courtship. Avoid only focusing on your partner. Look inward to find out if you are the one who needs to do the heavy lifting rather than your partner.

WHY IS COURTSHIP IMPORTANT?

- It has a higher success rate of leading to marriage: Many dating relationships last for relatively short periods of time, and end up going to nowhere. Hence a lot of people end up going through several relationships, most of which end up broken, often leaving emotional scars and wounds, spiritual and moral compromises, and several other negative consequences. However, due to its nature of serious commitment, often with a view to getting married, courtship relationships result in marriage much more successfully.

- It promotes peace when married:
  As God and godly principles are involved, and both partners take their time to work on themselves and on their relationship before getting married, such resulting marriages typically enjoy more peace and satisfaction

- Divorce rate is reduced to less than 0.001:
  Statistically, divorce is significantly reduced in marriages that result from courtship than those from dating relationships.

- It promotes unity, love and trust before and during marriage and reduces confusion:
  As a result of the understanding and trust that is built during courtship, stress of misunderstandings is typically much less in the marriage. Everything is made clear from the start how their lives and relationship should run and that reduces confusion.

- Able to withstand storm and overcome it together:

Better and stronger bonds are developed through courtship. That puts a marriage in a better place to withstand challenges that typically arise in marriages. Stronger and deeper foundation result in studdier and more enduring marriages

- Promotes closeness and togetherness:

  The bible says two shall become one. Understanding this words and building on it during courtship helps to promote

WHAT IS THE DURATION FOR COURTSHIP?

How long courtship should last depend on some factors such as:

- **THE AGE:** The age is one of the factors that affect the duration of courtship. Nowadays, children as young as elementary school agers are already into dating relationships. This is not proper. Relationships are supposed to be engaged in by individuals with some degree of life skills, physical, emotional, and spiritual maturity. Consequently, courtship relationships should typically not be entered into before the latter stages of the teenage years. As such, the length of courtship may depend on the ages of the partners involved. If started at or near the end of teenage years, courtship may take more than 3years. However, if the relationship starts at an older age, from 22years and above, it may require less than 3years. For preteens and midteens, the best thing is to concentrate on your education and building up yourself before venturing into any relationship.

- **LEVEL OF UNDERSTANDING FROM BOTH PARTNERS:** Both partners need to study and know each other very well before they can be discussing marriage. They must understand that life is not only about love alone but it comes with sharing, support and sacrifice for each other and all other responsibilities such as caring and looking out for yourself and your partner, taking care of the home, job and children that come with it.
- **MATURITY:** It is the ability to handle the affairs of the home, themselves, each other, children, careers, extended families and bills. To be capable of doing all this you must have something to support yourself and your family such as a job or a business.

In conclusion, courtship should generally be at least one year but depending on the circumstances around your meeting such as to where, when and how also contribute to how long your courting will last?

HOW MANY TIMES CAN I GO THROUGH COURTSHIP BEFORE MARRIAGE?

All things being equal, courtship should be once. when God is involved in choosing the right partner it is once. Examples are when God made Eve for Adam, when Abraham's servant involved God in choosing the right partner for his master's son, God chose Rebecca for Isaac. Many people rush into relationships either not taking time to seek God's mind through prayers,or not patiently waiting to hear God's response. Consequently, such courtship may fail, necessitating new ones, hopefully, in which God's will and counsel is better sought, and due diligence is applied for success. Moreover, walking out of a courtship is better than ending up in a miserable marriage or divorce.

Once you discover that the relationship cannot work, it is better you cut it off than to try to manage what you already know will not work right in the end. The bible says, "Can two people walk together except they agree? (Amos 3:3). If there are too many disagreements in choices you both make, things you both do and too many compromises from compulsion and your partner is not ready to let you both work it out then it is better to say goodbye to the relationship than marry and get divorce.

WHY DO I NEED TO ABSTAIN FROM SEX BEFORE MARRIAGE (FORNICATION)?

There are several important reasons fornication should not be involved or permitted before marriage. Fornication is defined as having sexual intercourse with your partner before marriage.

* * Firstly, sexual relationship is designed by God Himself between a man and a woman in marriage, restricted exclusively to the confines of marriage. "Marriage is honourable in all, and the bed undefiled" (Hebrew 13:4).

* However, breaking God's law regarding sex and marriage brings with it a plethora of detrimental consequences.

* It often becomes the focal point of the relationship, stunting the emotional, social, and spiritual areas of intimacy needed to grow equally for a long-term marriage.

* It clouds your judgment about certain issues and decision making.

* The scripture says, "Flee from sexual immorality for all other sins a person commits are outside the body but whoever sins

sexually, sins against their own body." (1corinthians 6:18). It is a commandment.

It is said "that your body is the temple of the holy spirit who is in you whom you have received from God" (1corinthians 6:19). If you are a child of God and He dwells in you, you must keep your body holy because God cannot dwell in an unholy place. Therefore you have to stay away from fornication that makes man unholy and makes one uninhabitable for God. The Bible tells us to "Present our bodies as a living sacrifice, holy, acceptable unto God (Romans 12:1).

Here are other scriptures regarding sexual purity: Matthew 15:19, 1 Corinthians 6:9, revelation 17:1-5, Galatians 5:19, 1 Corinthians 6:13, 1 Corinthians 7:2, 1 Corinthians 5:1, Ephesians 5:5, Colossians 3:5, Hebrew 12:16.

WHAT IS THE PREVENTIVE MEASURE AGAINST FORNICATION?

- To have the knowledge and understanding according to the Bible that sex is not permitted before marriage

- Just flee it; don't flirt with it. The bible says, "Flee from youthful lusts." (1 timothy 2:22). Fornication is sin therefore God advises us to flee.

Practical Steps

- Be in public places like libraries, restaurants, parks or be chaperone by a third person. Always arrange your meetings or being together in a public place. Never arrange meetings together in secluded places such as your house alone or in a room.
- Do not engage in sexual texting or chatters, either physically or on social media. No sending of sexual pictures to each other too.
- Don't watch sexual movies to prevent unnecessary sexual arousal.
- Don't live in the same house with your partner before marriage.
- Don't chat with your partner in your partner's room alone to avoid temptation.
- Be disciplined and keep your emotions in check.

  Ask God daily to help you withstand the temptation of fornication and the holy spirit to give you the strength to suppress your sexual needs until marriage.

ARE THERE REMEDIES FOR ME WHO ALREADY HAD SEX BEFORE MARRIAGE?

What can i do if i am already involved in sex before marriage? Or is it just too late for me? What next, now that i have realized that sex before marriage is a great sin before God?

The Bible says, for all have sin and come short of the glory of God. It is also written that if you do not conceal your sin but accept that you have sinned and confess it, ask God to forgive you and never to go back to sinning. The bible tells us that God is such a faithful and merciful God, ready to forgive and blot out our sins with the blood of Jesus Christ, His only begotten Son. Jesus paid the penalty for our sins when He laid down His life for us, that you and I could obtain and live a new life.

What are the steps you need to take?

- You must first make up your own mind to totally abstain from sexual desire till marriage because you realise now that it is sin and unacceptable before God.
- Then base on your decision to forsake the sin, go to God and ask Him for forgiveness and never to go back to sinning.
- Talk to your partner about your decision and see if your partner can do the same. Also make the sacrifice together to abstain from sex till marriage.
- If your partner is not ready to stop the sexual thing and wait till marriage you move on with your life. It is a personal life decision which you must make although it will hurt initially, but in the end it produces joy. The scripture says, "carry your cross and follow me". Mathew 16:24.
- And wait on the lord to make a way for you.

MORE THINGS TO ASK AND TALK ABOUT DURING COURTSHIP

In settling with a life partner in marriage you need to pay attention both to the "content" and the "container". "Content" here refers to what your partner is made up of, with respect to beliefs, conducts, habits, etc, the essential, yet the immaterial elements. While the "container" is the outward things that the eyes can perceive, such as the appearances and dressings. Both the inner as well as the external factors are essential. However, pondering some of the following questions can help give you better insights into the personality of the other person, thereby facilitating better discovery, assessment, and evaluation or your compactibility as potential marriage partners.

1. **BACKGROUNDS:**

    It is important to keep in mind that both of you are coming from different cultures and different backgrounds. The way you were raised and how things are done in your families and homes were most likely different. Therefore, you both need to ask questions and assess your backgrounds together and how the differences in upbringings could be amicably handled without causing interference in your relationship and after marriage. Discuss how to deal with the disparities in upbringing and experiences,so that they do not negatively affect your relationship and rob it of its health and success. For example your father helps your mum pack her plates and wash the dishes but your partner mum does the packing and washing of the dishes, dad relaxes. This could most likely cause different expectations in your marriage, if not discussed.

2. THE INTELLIGENCE LEVEL OF EDUCATION AND SPIRITUAL STATUS: What does she understand by submission to her husband, and what does he understand by love and respect for his wife? What level of education does each of you have? How much of God's words do you or your partner have and how much more are you willing to acquire together?

3. VACATION:

Do you enjoy taking vacation? Will there be vacation or not after marriage? Where and when do you want to have the vacation, putting into consideration how much money you are planning to put aside for vacation?

4. WHAT IF YOU GET PREGNANT WHEN NOT EXPECTED OR PLANNED FOR AFTER MARRIAGE: What is his view if after marriage and both of you don't want to have a child anymore but you become pregnant (to abort or to keep it)? Note that abortion is committing murder which God does not approve of. Also, what type of family planning would you use and the safety measures?

5. CHILDBEARING VIEW:

What is your idea of bearing children immediately after wedding or wait for some years before you both start? How many children do you want, does their genders matter to you?

6. YOUR SOCIAL AND MENTAL PHILOSOPHY OF LIFE:

How do you view life socially and mentally? Do you share the same view or your partner's view is different from yours? Do you like to socialize with people, meet new people?

7. WHAT IS YOUR VIEW ABOUT SMOKING, ALCOHOL AND DRUGS:
As Christian do you believe in little or no smoking compared to the word of God? What is your belief in drinking wine but not getting drunk or no wine at all?

8. THE AMOUNT OF INVOLVEMENT WITH IN-LAW:

How far and how much our parents and extended family will interfere when you get married. For example, will any of the family members come and live with you or you do not want them around, do they have to call before visiting? how often should their visit be?

9. TALK ABOUT SENSE OF HUMOR:

Are you someone who is always serious or friendly? Are you the reserved type that does not talk too much or you are the social type that likes friends and family around you? Are you the outgoing type or the person who wants to stay home and enjoy the comfort of being at home?

10. MARRIED BEFORE OR NOT:

Have any of you been married before? yes/no. If the answer is yes then to who, did you have children with that person, what brought about the separation? ? Ask questions.

11. PUNCTUALITY:

Are you someone who is always late or on time? If you are the late person you can begin your preparation two hours ahead of time. Are you the person that likes to make an appearance at an occasion late or early?

12. INTERDEPENDENCE:

Are you the type that wants your partner to be totally dependent on you for food, shelter and all expenses or you want your partner to work and be independent? Do you want to be a sole responsible person in the family, or you want to share the responsibilities? What is the ratio of responsibility if there is any?

13. ASK IF THERE IS A WAY FOR VERBAL INTIMACY:

Women like to talk, to share the event of their day with their spouse to also be told how beautiful they are and how they are loved. Are you someone who comes back from work and sits at the TV and does not like talking? Can someone express their feelings to you without criticizing or judging? One of the gifts a man can give to a woman is the ability for her to express her feelings without fear.

14. ROLE OF HOW TO RESOLVE CONFLICT:

No matter how much in-love you are or will be, you will have disagreements over issues, probably as a result of difference in perspectives on certain issues or differences in manner of handling things. How and when you resolve such disagreements or conflicts is very important. Listening to one another and making efforts to work through things without anger, resentment or fight is important in conflict resolution. Ask your partner what are the things you could do that he/she would not be able to tolerate. What are your fears, what could that person do that you might feel like divorcing each other? When he/she gets angry what can you do to appease your partner or what will your partner do to increase the anger? What are the particular words that will make you angry or should not be used when angry? What body languages would get your partner angry the more. How easily do you forgive and forget offences? (Jesus said after 70 times 7 a person sin against you before you do not forgive; Matthew 18:21-22). Talk about them and use the bible as your standard.

15. YOUR LEVEL OF AMBITION:

There is a place for vision and ambition, talk about it. What do you want to achieve in your life, how can you support each other's dreams to a higher height without breaking or affecting your home?

16. HOW SHOULD YOU HANDLE FRIENDSHIP WITH THE OPPOSITE GENDER?

Can you claim that you love your partner and yet touch another woman/man in the wrong places? Should you hug-tight another male/female? When you are married will you have friends that are not my friends?

17. RELIGION, SPIRITUAL BELIEFS AND PREFERENCES:

Make your partner understand that no matter how much you love your partner there is a place that God has in your life that your partner can never have. So, anyone that says he/she loves you and not your God please walk away as fast as you can from that relationship. Are we compatible in our beliefs? Will your God be my God, will we be going to the same church to fellowship or separate churches? Will you make God and His word guide us throughout our lives together?

18. YOU MUST HAVE A MULTIDIMENSIONAL RELATIONSHIP:

There is a place in your heart that your parents will have in your life that your partner can not have. They are forever respected and honored. Is your partner ready to accept your parents as part of your life or separate you from them completely after marriage, not to care for them, not to call them and they are not allowed to call you. Will there be a place for friends in your family? How much of external friendship will be permissible or welcome?

19. ATTITUDE ABOUT WEIGHT GAIN OR LOSS:

If you want to have a good idea of what your partner is going to look like in future as far as weight is concerned, you need to take a look at her mum/his father. To an extent seeing her mother/ his father might give you a rough estimation of how she is going to be in future. Is he likely to develop a pot-belly later in life? If your partner has a condition or stipulation that if you get fat he wouldn't be able to handle it, tell him you will do your best. But let him know that in the event that hormones take over, will he still be there to love and appreciate you. This issue of weight gain and change in body condition has destroyed marriages. Be sure to talk about it.

20. ABOUT CHURCH INVOLVEMENT:

What is your church activity and involvement going to be like? Will it be only Sunday to Sunday involvement or other church activities. How involved will you be after marriage?

21. HOBBIES AND INTEREST:

Accepting your partner's hobbies especially those that are good like watching football, drawing etc. helps to enhance the relationship. Participating in some of his or her hobbies if not all makes your relationship stronger and draws you both closer. For example, if your partner loves watching football, join him to watch it together. If the lady loves watching movies instead of news, join her to watch together once in a while. I do not support the opinion that someone should be forced to give up his or her hobbies, especially the healthy ones that do not bring harm to the relationship.

Everyone has his or her peculiar interest. Try and find out what your partner is. By supporting and developing each other's interests, you boost your confidence in yourselves and for each other. Never discard or take your partner's interest for granted. Take your partner's interest as special and important as yours.

23. **TYPE OF MUSIC ENJOY LISTENING TO:**

Even though they are born again, some listen to classical music and Christian music, while others "no" to all other kinds of music besides Christian music. Talk about it.

24. **YOUR PHYSICAL APPEARANCE:**

As much as your inner beauty matters you must also take care of your physical body. Bathe regularly, dress neatly and nicely. Dress appropriately for different occasions. Do not over do it with your physical body.

25. **INCOME TO BE SPENT AND SAVED:**

Who keeps money? Do you want a joint account, separate or both? How much money to be allocated for vacation, clothing, bills, extended families and so on? How much money to be given away and to whom, the degree of risk to be taken with investments?

26. CLEANLINESS:

How clean are you? Do you throw your stuff all over the place or are you well organized? Cleanliness of your home, clothes, body and everything in general is vital. The Bible says, "cleanliness is next to Godliness."

27. WAYS OF HANDLING SICKNESS:

Do you believe in divine healing without medication, while your partner does not mind using medication? Ask and talk about your approach to health and wellbeing.

28. INTERPERSONAL AND SOCIAL SKILLS: What interpersonal skills do your potential spouse have? Is he or she a people person, or prideful and condescending? Evaluate his or her ability to relate with others.

29. GEOGRAPHICAL AREA: Where do you want to live when you marry, what type, size and style of house do you want to live in, what type of furniture and decorations you want in your home? You need to ask and talk about them especially if you have a partner with expensive taste.

CONCLUSION

In conclusion, attempting to make your relationship and marriage work without the involvement of God is like the builder who builds in vain without God building the house - Psalms 127:1-2,Matthew 7:24-27 . You need to invite and give your life to Jesus Christ who has paid the price for your sins on the cross and came to help you to succeed. He will be your guide and support whenever and wherever you need His help in your life. He will help you build a healthy and lasting relationship.

If you are ready, say this short prayer: Lord Jesus, I open up my heart to you and I invite you in as my lord and saviour today. Forgive all my past sins and wash me clean with your precious blood. From today, I will involve you to help me build my life and my relationship. Thank you Jesus for accepting me. In Jesus name I pray. Amen.

If you did say this prayer, I welcome into the family of Happy people. I encourage you to look for a church to fellowship where the word of God is being preached and practiced to assist you know and grow more in the Lord.

www.ingramcontent.com/pod-product-compliance
Lightning Source LLC
LaVergne TN
LVHW041552060526
838200LV00037B/1254